UNIVERSITY THEOLOGY THEMES

GOD EXISTS

The Biblical Record of God's Self-Revelation

THOMAS BARROSSE, C.S.C.

University of Notre Dame Press
1963

Nihil Obstat:

       Reverend Frederick Barr, C.S.C.
       Censor librorum

Imprimatur:

       ✠ Leo A. Pursley, D.D.
       Bishop of Fort Wayne-South Bend

© 1963 by

UNIVERSITY OF NOTRE DAME PRESS

Library of Congress Catalog Card
Number: 63-15346

GOD EXISTS

ANCIENT NON-ISRAELITE IDEAS OF DIVINITY

The study of comparative religions shows us the peoples of all primitive cultures aware of power and reality completely beyond their control, even their full understanding. We might style this reality "the sacred" or "the wholly other." As instances of its manifestations, primitive man grouped together the most varied phenomena. For example, he placed weather phenomena there: the frightening storm and the devastating flood, well able to destroy him or his possessions; also the seasonal recurrence of the earth's fertility, so important for his food supply. There, too, he placed physiological and psychological phenomena, such as diseases and dreams and, to the degree that he may have known them, extrasensory perception and mystical experience. He even placed there certain momentous events far back in his dimly remembered past — events of which he still felt the effects, such as the organization of the tribe or tribal confederacy to which he belonged or the founding of the village in which he lived.

We find all primitives in possession of practices or rites by which they attempt to align themselves — indeed, their whole profane world — with the sacred and its presence, or with its interventions in their lives. As they become more sophisticated, however, they tend to conceptualize the sacred, to conceive of it after the manner of powers or realities with which they are familiar, and to interpret their rites as means of protecting themselves against these powers or of rendering or keeping them helpful or, finally, of communicating with them. They have rites to ward off or cure diseases, to insure the fertility of the soil and to communicate with the past act of the founding of their tribe or tribal confederacy and so reinforce the bonds holding their society together. It is often hard to decide in any given primitive culture precisely how far conceptualization of the sacred has proceeded and how far the primitive rites have degenerated into magic.

In the conceptualizing process, primitive man quite naturally tended to personify these powers or realities — that is, to conceive of them after his own likeness, conveying on them not only the power to know and to will but even the passions, the likes and dislikes and all the other properties of the human person — and to treat them accordingly. When he became more civilized, these personifications simply grew more sophisticated.

The land between the Tigris and Euphrates rivers, where a complex civilization had developed well before 2000 B.C., illustrates this point very well. In Mesopotamia, as the ancient Greeks called it, the various great powers or realities of nature had been personified and were revered and invoked. *Shamash* (sun) was either the material heavenly body which gave light and heat to man's earth or the same heavenly body invoked for guidance and help. *Anu* (sky) was either the solid bright-blue or night-black dome of the heavens on which ancient man gazed, or the beneficent and mighty protector who continually sent down blessings upon him. *Tiamat* (deep or chaos) was at once the impersonal disorder and darkness from which the ordered world of man had emerged and the fearful female enemy who threatened to re-engulf man's world at the occurrence of great natural catastrophes.

In reading ancient Mesopotamian texts we cannot always be sure whether the authors are speaking of the natural realities in themselves or treating them after the manner of human persons. However, passage from one way of speaking to the other posed no problem for these authors, because the ancient Mesopotamian simply saw no need to make a distinction between the two.

Gradually, these personifications not only grew more numerous, but each had various functions and a fairly consistent set of attributes assigned to it. *Ishtar,* for example, presided over love and fertility and assured the yearly recurrence of spring. *Ea* presided over wisdom and learning and was held responsible for the existence of that which struck the ancients as most ingenious, such as the making of man. Nevertheless, it is not clear that these personifications ever became full *persons* in the minds of their devotees — individuals capable of knowing and loving, completely dissociated from the physical powers or realities with which they were connected.

These last examples have already brought into the context of the ancient Near East our examination of primitive man's awareness and personification of powers above his understanding and control. We must now examine more directly and thoroughly this awareness and its development among the peoples of those lands.

The family of languages — the so-called Semitic tongues — spoken by most of the people of ancient Mesopotamia and their neighbors to the west and south (the tribes of the Syrian and Arabian deserts and the peoples that lived along the eastern coast of the Mediterranean Sea) possesses a root used quite frequently to designate the personified powers or realities of which we have been treating, a root that appears in Hebrew as 'el (pronounced approximately like the English "ale") or 'elōah (ĕ-lō'-ah). In all likelihood the root originally meant "to be mighty" or "powerful" or possibly "to be above" and, therefore, could readily serve to designate the "powers above" man's comprehension or control. Though its derivation differs, this Semitic expression corresponds rather exactly to the ancient Latin term deus (deriving probably from the ancient Indo-European word for "sky"), from which we get our English words "deity" and "divine." The very term the ancient Semites employed, then, shows that their idea of deity implied its *transcendence* or superiority in relation to man.

We must not, of course, feel that this note of superiority ever put the ancient Semite at the complete mercy of his god. Primitive man's attempts to protect himself from superior powers, or to keep them favorable, turned into an elaborate system of magical rites in highly civilized ancient Egypt. Mesopotamia also had these practices. Sacrifice, in particular, was looked upon as nourishment which deities fed upon and enjoyed; the offerer could, therefore, allay their hostility or secure their favor. In fact, many considered prayer and sacrifice as needs of the deities; and they felt that the gods had created men to supply these needs and services. Even in the second millennium before Christ, when ancient Near Eastern religion reached perhaps its highest development — when the most beautiful descriptions of the cosmic might and majesty of the gods were being composed — these notions of deity's dependence on man or of man's ability to influence and, to some degree, control deity remained generally acceptable. If, then, we recognize transcendence as a fundamental note of the ancient Semitic idea of deity, we must hastily add that it is definitely a limited superiority.

When written records become numerous enough to construct a fairly continuous history of the Semitic peoples, we find them speaking of numerous *'elim* (ā-lēm´) or *'elohim* (ĕ-lō-hēm´), to use the

Hebrew plurals. Regularly, however, each group
(for example, each tribe or city) had its special *'el*
with whom it had particular ties. This fact has led
certain historians of religion to surmise that most
Semitic groups originally had each a single deity —
the deity peculiarly connected with a great ancestor
or with its place of origin — and that only later did
they accept a plurality of gods: for example, by
accepting those of neighbors with whom they became socially involved by conquest, treaty, trade or
like association. This position is hardly more than
conjecture, however, since the pre-eminence of a
particular deity is perhaps no more readily explained as an indication of some sort of primitive
monotheism than as a result of an important historical occurrence (the deity's peculiar association
with some influential person — a village founder,
for example — or a momentous event in their
past).

For our purposes, this question of the earlier
Semitic ideas about the unity or multiplicity of
divinity has little importance. Suffice it to note that
when the ancestors of the people of Israel, Abraham, Isaac, and Jacob, appeared about 1800 B.C.,
the various groups of the Semitic world all recognized a plurality of *'elohim*. They were all poly-
theists with their pantheons or boards of deities,
each charged with a variety of functions in govern-
ing the world of man and all presided over by a
chief god. In the pantheon of Syria-Palestine, to

which the Hebrew patriarchs migrated from Mesopotamia, the chief deity (a rather shadowy and distant figure whose only exclusive prerogatives seem to have been creation and the presidency of the pantheon) had arrogated to himself the title *'El* while the most popular was *Baal* (*bā'-al,* a west Semitic word meaning "lord" or "master"), a deity of rain and fertility. Each of them had a consort: *Asherah* (*a-shē'-ra*) was El's and *Anat* (*a-nat'*), the virgin deity of war, Baal's. Along with transcendence, then, we can also list *multiplicity* as a regular note of the Semitic concept of deity, although with a definite tendency to favoring one or a few of the gods either as head of the pantheon or as most popular.

Baal illustrates quite well the rather fluid character of the personality of the ancient Semitic gods. In one of the Baal myths of ancient Ugarit (a large city on the Mediterranean coast just south of the modern Turkish-Syrian frontier), the god meets death and all fertility fails; he then resuscitates and fertility returns. Is the myth (and the god in the myth) really anything more than a personification of the yearly return and recession of infertile winter? Were the god really independent of and distinct from the fertility over which he presides, surely some other deity could supply it in his absence. Furthermore, we meet with frequent references to the Baal of this location or that — for example, the Baal of Peor (the place where the Hebrews fell into pagan worship according to Numbers 25) or Baal Zebul (the Prince), the god of the city of Ekron according to II Kings 1:2. Accordingly, various Old Testament books speak of a plurality of Baals. Such a way of speaking would seem to preclude the conception of Baal as a person and to reduce the god to a power manifesting itself or invoked at this or that sanctuary and merely personified — that is, merely conceived of and treated after the manner of human persons. Hence, to transcendence and multiplicity we may add the tendency towards *personalization* as a further mark of the ancient Semitic notion of deity, adding however that it never seems to have succeeded in really turning the gods into persons.

We may perhaps also add *goodness* as a final note of the ancient Near Eastern idea of godhead. But here, too, we must qualify. If man depended on deity, certainly he hoped and prayed for divine benevolence. He even expected it — above all, once he had performed the required rituals to honor the god or had offered him sacrifices. In the same way he hoped for and expected protection and beneficence from his king or ruler. Naturally, in the latter case his expectation often proved false; so also in the former. Natural forces often brought about destruction, and for no apparent reason. The deities who were personifications of these forces could not escape the charge of fickleness — all the more since human persons, none of whom are

of Melchizedek, king of Salem, identified with Abraham's God in Genesis 14:22, is *'El 'Elyon* (El Most High). When in the southern Palestinian desert God speaks to the fugitive Hagar sending her back to her mistress, Abraham's wife (16:13), the slave-girl calls Him *'El Roi* ("El who sees" or "who appears"). With Abimelech, Abraham swears an alliance at Beersheba and then plants a tamerisk tree to serve as a memorial of the event; it becomes the shrine of *El 'Olam* (El of Eternity), probably the God invoked in the oath (22:21-34). In reference to the apparition he has at Bethel (28:12f.) Jacob names the sanctuary he later erects there (35:7) *'El Bethel* ("El of Bethel" or perhaps "El [called] Bethel"), and in 31:13 he receives a divine communication in Mesopotamia from the same El of Bethel (with an explicit reference to the earlier apparition). In the great divine communication of chapter 17, in which God promises Abraham that his descendants will possess the entire land of Canaan, He identifies Himself to the patriarch (v. 1) as *'El Shaddai* (probably "El of the Mountains," perhaps in the sense of "El Most Exalted"); then in 35:11f., He makes the same promise to Jacob identifying Himself in the same way and referring, at least implicitly, to the earlier promise. In 28:3f., Isaac, and in 48:3f., Jacob, speak of *'El Shaddai* with undeniable allusions to the earlier promise.

The presence of "El" as principal element in all these divine names makes the reader feel that it is the same God who appears in each of these accounts. When, however, he notes that each name except the last (El Shaddai) is associated with a particular locality, and the last with the particular divine communication of a specific promise to Abraham, he cannot help wondering whether the patriarchs did not speak of the El of this or that locality or of this or that theophany as the Canaanites spoke of the Baal of this or that shrine. In other words, if they conceived of El as a single divinity, it is not at all clear that they *completely* dissociated Him from the Canaanite El, or that they thought of Him as a *full person* rather than as a power manifesting itself benevolently at this or that shrine in this or that place after the manner of a person.

Perhaps the most that we can deduce from the accounts in Genesis 12-50 about the patriarchs' idea of their God is the following hypothesis, admittedly a somewhat tenuous hypothesis because based on a relatively scant and sketchy collection of stories handed down orally for centuries — certainly with remarkable fidelity, yet doubtless tailored somewhat in the process to bring out their religious import for the people who retold them. We would suggest, then, that they felt that a divinity, that is, a superior power, manifesting itself to them here and there in Canaan, was directing their movements to the ultimate good of their descendants. Whether they looked upon Him as personal in the full sense of this word is by no means clear. They distinguished

Him from other deities (at least from one other deity according to 31:53), but whether they wholly distinguished Him from the Canaanite El is not certain. The way in which they distinguished Him from other deities would seem to imply that they took the existence of these other deities for granted; whether or not they did so, we have no indication that they had anything to do with them. The evidence indicates rather that the El who had brought Abraham out of Mesopotamia to Canaan was the only Divinity that received their worship. (We may ask, however, whether the same sort of monolatry did not obtain among other contemporary groups — for example, in the family of Laban as reported in 31:51-53.)[3] Hence, the God of the patriarchs appears as transcendent, and one in more or less the same way as the divinities of the ancient Near East in general.

There *is,* however, something different about Him — very different — and this founds the unique relationship of the Hebrew patriarchs to Him. The difference lies in His goodness. He did not simply do good to the patriarchs as other divinities did good to

---

[3] Something should be said about the difficult problem of the "messenger of Yahweh" (usually rendered "angel of the Lord") and the "members of the elohim" (usually rendered "sons of God"). The former expression is quite ancient and seems to refer not to angels in the later sense of the term but to the apparition Yahweh used to communicate with men. The latter expression is later and probably expresses the Israelite belief in angels. Note, however, that these are not former polytheistic deities demoted to a lower rank. During the earlier period of Israelite religion Yahweh was not conceived of as having a heavenly court. He was not only without companion deities but even without superhuman servants.

their devotees — Baal sending rain and fertility, for
example. He is the God of a promise — a promise
concerning the distant future of their descendants.
The patriarchs had to accept His word and wait
upon its fulfillment. He, therefore, became a God
directing history — and their relationship to Him
was one of faith and trust.[4]

THE GOD OF MOSES AND THE
PRE-MONARCHY PERIOD

Of the four or more centuries that the patriarchs'
descendants spent in Egypt we know practically
nothing. Our information takes up again on the eve
of their departure.

The exodus and the desert-wanderings that followed it, dominated by the heroic figure of Moses,
constitute the experience that made the most profound impression upon Israel's national memory.
The account is preserved in the national epic found
(interpolated with much legal material) in the
Books of Exodus and Numbers. A reading of these
books, especially the former, reveals why the people
set such value on this period: in the desert into
which they had fled, Moses mediated for the motley
horde of fugitives a covenant with the God Yahweh,
who in accord with His promise then led their
forces into the land of Canaan and served as their

---

[4] On the uniqueness of the Judeo-Christian ideas of God as a
God of history and of faith as an integral part of religion, cf.
Mircea Eliade, *The Myth of the Eternal Return* (New York: Pan-
theon, 1954); also in paperback, *Cosmos and History* (New York:
Harper [Torch Book # 50], 1959).

source of unity while they took the territory from its inhabitants. It was this desert experience, therefore, which gave them existence as a unified people and inspired them to occupy the land in which their history would unfold.

Many scholars feel that the Books of Exodus and Numbers oversimplify (as oft-retold stories are wont to do), that not all Israel took part in the exodus, but that several of the tribes (especially the northern ones) had never left Canaan. In any case, there can be little doubt that the group which came out of Egypt brought the religion of Yahweh into Canaan. Moreover, this religion of Yahweh provided the cornerstone of unity for the confederacy of Israelite tribes during the two centuries after the exodus before the people had a king. The epic of the exodus and desert days finds its sequel in the account of these two centuries contained in the collection of the memories of the great heroes of the pre-monarchy period, found in the Books of Joshua and Judges. Archeology and other sciences of the past can furnish us little direct information about the person of Moses and later Israelite champions. However, they provide us with extensive knowledge of the times and frequent confirmation of the more notable events mentioned in the Old Testament books with which we are concerned (like details of Egyptian persecution of foreign minorities or the destruction of Canaanite cities by invaders). So abundant is the evidence that to deny the sub-

stantially historical character of the accounts is quite
unreasonable.

What was the notion of their God that the people
of Israel formed from their encounter with Him in
the desert? How did this conception fare during the
pre-monarchy days in Canaan?

That the religion of Moses makes a definite
advance over the past — even a break with it —
stands most clearly indicated by the new name
which the God of Moses has: Yahweh. In two
independent accounts, the Book of Exodus shows
God revealing Himself to the deliverer of Israel
under this name (3:13ff.; 6:2ff.). Though in
both texts He identifies Himself with the God
(*Elohim*) of the patriarchs or with El Shaddai,
whom the patriarchs revered, He also makes quite
clear in both that the ancestors did not know Him
as Yahweh. In fact, scholars have been unable to
turn up a single clear indication of Yahweh-worship
before the time of Moses. To take but one illustra-
tion: though Semitic personal names are usually
sentences and regularly contain a theophoric element (El or the name of some specific divinity —
for example, the name of Abraham's son, Ishmael,
"God hears"), not a single instance of a name containing Yahweh had been found before Moses' time
either in the Old Testament or outside it. But from
his time they abound (for example, Eli*jah*, "Yahweh is my God," *Jeho*shaphat, "Yahweh has
judged," etc.).

If, however, we look to the meaning of this divine name to ascertain what is new in Moses' appreciation of God, we find ourselves forced to resort to hypothesis and conjecture. It is generally agreed (though scattered scholars dissent) that the name Yahweh derives from the Aramaic or archaic Hebrew verb *hawah*, "to be." Some have suggested that the form (unfortunately ambiguous) is causative and means "the one who makes to be," that is, "creator." Professor William F. Albright has even conjectured that it might have come from a litany of patriarchal times: "El Shaddai, who makes to be the hosts of heaven, . . . the armies of Israel," etc.[5] Others have suggested that it is the simple form of the verb and means "the one who is" as opposed to the impotent deities of Israel's neighbors (who "are not") or "the one who is what He is," that is, the all-transcendent one who cannot be described in human language. All of these hypotheses are possible. All of them refer to Yahweh's superiority or transcendence as regards the world of man (creator), other gods (who "are not"), or man's powers of comprehension (the ineffable). All of these notions were actually predicated of Yahweh in later epochs. But it is not at all clear that any one of them was affirmed of Him during the Mosaic period. A final opinion interprets the divine name as "the one who is there," or "the one who is present," and refers it to Yahweh's con-

[5] See *From the Stone Age to Christianity* (New York: Double-day [Anchor], 1957), pp. 15 f.

tinuous presence in Israel to fulfill His part of the
Sinai covenant. This position has the distinct advantage of associating the new divine name with the
new relationship of God and Israel: the covenant;
but we may question whether the verb "to be" can
mean "to be present" or "to be there" without the
addition of an adverb.

Whatever the precise meaning of the name, the
way in which it is used shows the newness of the
idea of God which accompanied its introduction. In
the first place, it is not connected with any particular natural force — as Baal, for example, was with
the rain and fertility. In the second, it is not connected with any particular place. There is no question of a Yahweh of this or that locality; or even
of this or that apparition as there was of Baal of
Peor, a Baal of Ekron; or even an El of Salem and
an El of Bethel in patriarchal times. His name never
occurs with a genitive except in the title Yahweh
Sebaoth, taken by many as a contraction of the
fuller "Yahweh, God of [Israel's or heaven's] hosts."
True, Yahweh is the God who manifested Himself
at Sinai, but the covenant He made there is by no
means restricted to that locality. He accompanies
His people into the land of promise and is ever
active among them; thus they feel no need to modify
His name according as His saving self-manifestations occur in this place or that. Finally, He is not
even bound to His people by any necessary, un-

breakable bond. The covenant is bilateral. He, not Israel, took the initiative in making it. He does not need the people's service. If they do not observe their part of the bargain, He will repudiate it. In short, Yahweh is one with a unity independent of the forces of nature, of any local or temporal self-manifestations, and even of the people of His covenant — a divine unity which we find hard to match in the ancient Near East. Though the term does not occur to describe Him, this independence seems sufficient to constitute Him a *person* in the full sense of the word.

Whether His difference from earlier deities excludes the very existence of other gods is another question. The Old Testament books which contain the accounts of the Mosaic and immediately post-Mosaic periods speak of the gods of other peoples. Nowhere do they explicitly deny the existence of these foreign gods. There are even passages in which Israelites clearly seem to take their existence for granted. For example, in Judges 11:24 Jephthah demands that the Ammonites renounce their designs on Israelite territory, "Do you not occupy the land that your God Chemosh gave to you? Shall we not occupy all the land that our God Yahweh has taken away from its owners?" On the other hand, the Old Testament writings on the pre-monarchy days do underscore a characteristic of Yahweh which sets Him in active opposition to the other deities: His intolerance of them, His "jealousy." Repeatedly, in both the desert days and the time of the Judges, Yahweh vigorously punished the apostasy of His people. It is quite unlikely that the repeated infidelities which brought down disaster after disaster on the people were their total repudiation of the God of the Sinai covenant. They could hardly have been more than the people's attempts to render service to the local divinities *along with* their own God. But Yahweh would not tolerate such divided loyalty.

The God of Israel is repeatedly called a "jealous God" in texts whose content, and perhaps whose very words go back to the days of the desert wanderings — for example, the first commandment of the Decalogue: "You must have no other gods besides me. . . . You must not bow down before them or serve them, for I Yahweh your God am a jealous God. . . ." Hence, whatever may be said about Israelite ideas regarding the existence of other gods besides Yahweh in the Mosaic period, the people found themselves bound to a *practical monotheism*. And this phenomenon seems to be a unique mark of Israelite religion in the ancient world.

Yahweh differed from other gods in yet another way. We have already seen that certain interpreters understand His name as an affirmation of His transcendence. Whether or not the name carries that meaning, Yahweh's transcendence was grasped

and the appreciation of it expressed in a rather un-
usual way. We must be careful not to exaggerate.
The pagan Near East, during the second millennium
before Christ, exhibited a pronounced tendency to
treat the gods as cosmic forces rather than local or
national personifications of those forces, and literary
compositions appeared exalting their worldwide
greatness and power.[6] Little or none of such literature appeared concerning Yahweh until the first
millennium. On the other hand, in the worship of the
pagan gods the use of images held an important
place; in Mosaic religion all images were forbidden.
Exodus 20:4 lists this prohibition among the precepts of the Decalogue, and the archeologist's spade
has failed to this day to turn up a single image of
Yahweh from any orthodox Israelite source. Not
that the pagans never conceived their gods as in-
visible: at times the god Hadad, often depicted as
standing upright upon the back of a bull, is apparently conceived of as invisibly present astride a
sculptured riderless bull. But Yahweh is *always* in-
visible, and no image may ever serve to represent
Him — an apparently unique phenomenon in
ancient Semitic religion.

Yahweh differed from other deities in His total
independence from natural forces and His greater
independence from time and place. He differed in

[6] Cf. the beautiful Egyptian hymn to the sun god dating from
about 1370 B.C. and translated in J. B. Pritchard, *Ancient Near
Eastern Texts Relating to the Old Testament* (Princeton, N. J.:
Princeton University Press, 1950), p. 34.

the jealousy which forced His worshippers into a
sort of practical monotheism. He differed in His
wholly imageless cult. In short, He differed in His
more marked personal character, His unity and His
transcendence. But He differed most of all in His
goodness.

We can understand this goodness in two senses:
as righteousness and as beneficence. In both senses
Yahweh's goodness is unique.

Righteousness is of the very essence of the covenant. In order to become and remain Yahweh's people, Israel had not only to worship Him alone but
also to observe the marvelous summary of fundamental social obligations which we call the Decalogue.[7] It is easy to say that the terms of the covenant necessarily had to assure the Israelites' fidelity
to one another (otherwise they could not be a united
people) and to Yahweh (otherwise they could not
be *His* people). But just as the divine intolerance of
other deities expressed in the first commandment is
unique, so the extraordinary summary of fundamental social duties found in the rest of the Decalogue has no ancient non-Israelite parallel.

Even more, the moral code assembled there was
observed by Yahweh Himself. The Semitic deities,
as we already have seen, had all the passions, faults,
and fickleness of men. They sometimes fought

[7] The first and second precepts of the Decalogue concern cult.
The third (on the sanctification of the Sabbath) concerns a day of
rest (not primarily a day of prayer) and is therefore a social in-
stitution. The remaining precepts all concern social obligations.

among themselves (for example, in the creation myth in which the creator god subdues the goddess of chaos). They frequently engaged in behavior that their devotees would have found reprehensible in human beings: mass slaughter of the innocent, debauchery, seduction, greed, and the like. The explanation lies, of course, in that they personified natural forces and their actions in the myths reflected the behavior of these forces. The fact remains, however, that they *did* engage in such behavior. Now early Israelite poets transferred to Yahweh much of the imagery used in the myths. In the ancient canticle in Exodus 15, which celebrates the crossing of the Sea, Yahweh drives back the waters with the breath of His nostrils and battles the pursuing Egyptians with the might of His arm. In the very old song of triumph in Judges 5, which hymns the victory of Deborah and Barak over the Canaanites, Yahweh's march makes mountains quake and clouds pour down rain. But in not a single passage does He act in a way that we might term unjust. Whenever He gives vent to anger, He is always enraged at man's injustice. Whenever He destroys or sends disaster, the reason is man's reprehensible behavior.

Yahweh does punish, but He is more prone to beneficence, especially to His people. In fact, we find this stated quite explicitly in the text of the Decalogue as preserved in Exodus 20. Yahweh identifies Himself as "a jealous God punishing child-

ren for the sins of their fathers to the third or fourth
generation" of those unfaithful to Him (v. 5).[8] But
He adds immediately that He shows "loyal attachment to the thousandth generation of His friends"
(v. 6). Or again, in the very primitive story in
Exodus 34, in which Moses asks for direct knowledge of Yahweh, the God of the covenant — so to
speak — defines Himself (vv. 6f.) as

> Yahweh, a God (El) tender and actively favor-
> ing, slow to anger and abounding in loyal attach-
> ment and fidelity, keeping His loyal attachment
> to the thousandth generation, forgiving abomina-
> tion, rebellion, and sin [the three terms used most
> often in the Old Testament for sin], but by no
> means leaving it unpunished, inflicting punish-
> ment for the abominations of parents on their
> children and grandchildren to the third and
> fourth generations.

The "tenderness" and "active favor" mentioned in
this latter passage are two of the most important
attributes of the good covenant God. The even more
important "loyal attachment" mentioned in both
texts, Yahweh's chief attribute, refers to His fidelity,
to His covenant.

    8 We regard punishment of children for their parents' sins as un-
just. The earlier Old Testament period considered it altogether right.
For them the family was a unit in a much stricter sense than for
us just as a nation was a unit much more strictly than for ourselves. In fact, man is a social animal, and the good fortune or
misfortune of individuals is closely bound up with that of others
even when those individuals have nothing whatever to say about it
(for example, a whole nation is involved in a war whether every
individual citizen wants it or not; a family suffers from ill-calculated
financial ventures of the father whether they know anything about
them or not).

Faithful observance of Yahweh's side of the covenant consisted not simply in protecting His people
but also, and even especially, in bringing them into
the land of Canaan and establishing them as its
owners. Like the God of the patriarchs, the God of
Moses is master of His people's history. Like the
patriarchs, their descendants must live in reliance on
the divine promise. Yahweh's goodness, then, is not
simply a general beneficence towards Israel but a
benevolence which shows itself in His management
of their history through several generations, and
which demands faith and trust on their part.

A personal God independent of natural forces,
of times and places, and even of the people of His
covenant; a God totally unwilling that His people
should worship any deity but Himself; a Divinity too
transcendent to be represented by any image; a
Deity consistently righteous as He demands His
people to be, and good to the point of directing their
entire history to their advantage — such was Yahweh as He revealed Himself to His people in their
desert encounter with Him.

THE PROPHETS' CONCEPTION OF GOD

The period of the monarchy forms the zenith of
pre-exilic Israelite history — especially the years of
David's reign and the earlier years of Solomon's
when Israel was an independent nation and could
boast a more than merely modest military prowess
and economic prosperity. Our knowledge of the

more than four centuries of Israelite monarchy
(1030-587 B.C.) is relatively detailed, more detailed than our knowledge of any other comparable
section of the entire Old Testament period. The
Bible furnishes us with most of its information on
the monarchy in the Books of Samuel and Kings.
Archeology has amply illustrated the biblical data
with Palestinian excavations, and has also supplied
extensive background in the recovery of abundant
contemporary Mesopotamian records.

We may divide the period into an initial abortive
attempt to establish the monarchy with Saul, the
highly successful reign of the wholehearted Yahwist
David along with the glorious earlier years of his
son and successor Solomon; and the separate king-
doms of Israel and Judah, originating as a result of
the dissatisfaction of the northern tribes with Solomon's absolutist rule, now faring well, now poorly
until they finally disappeared before the mounting
military might of Mesopotamian powers.

Already in the days of Saul and David the Israelite prophets began to exert a notable influence on
the history of God's people. The prophet Samuel
first anointed Saul king, then rejected him in Yahweh's name, and finally chose and anointed David
as his successor. The prophet Nathan promised
David in Yahweh's name a dynasty that would en-
dure. But it was especially during the days of the
divided monarchy that the prophets directed the

course of Israelite history and profoundly transformed Israelite religion.

Ecstatic bands, generally enjoying relatively low repute, either wandering about the countryside or attached to certain shrines, singing the praises of their god and giving oracles in his name for those who sought them — such were the prophets of ancient Syria-Palestine among the Israelites as well as among their pagan neighbors. But Israel's prophets — or at least many of them — especially during the monarchy period became quite different from their pagan counterparts. The ecstatic phenomena gradually grew less important and may even have completely ceased. From oracle-giving to private persons they turned to proclaiming publicly to king and people Yahweh's designs on the sinful partners to His covenant. In the face of all the opposition they met, they emphatically declared that they were sent by Yahweh and that they were determined to carry out their mission. It was what they learned about the God of the covenant from their own inner experience of Him that they proclaimed to the people, succeeding finally in bringing them to a much fuller appreciation of the God who was directing their history.

To appreciate the new understanding of Yahweh that Israel acquired from these men, we must trace its growth historically. In the days of David the Yahwism of the pre-monarchy period reached its most flourishing situation. As far as we can tell, the God of Israel and He alone was worshipped wholeheartedly by the king and apparently by the people as well. Complete masters of the land He had given them, they possessed to the full the prosperity and well-being they had expected from Him. Since David, at least through much of his reign, had little of the ancient Near Eastern absolute ruler about him, the full consequences of the substitution of a monarchy for the tribal confederacy remained hidden. When David's rule reached its glorious zenith, the prophet Nathan canonized his dynasty. Between Yahweh and the people of His covenant now stood a man — an imperfect man at that — through whom Yahweh would henceforth bestow prosperity on Israel.

The tragic potentialities of the kingship became apparent during Solomon's reign (970-922 B.C.). This absolute monarch imposed taxes and forced labor on the freedom-loving Israelites. He divided the country into administrative districts that disregarded tribal boundaries and so offended tribal sensibilities. He introduced the commerce that would lead to the breakdown of their agricultural way of life and to the growth of an ever-richer merchant class that would gradually exploit and dispossess the small landholders of pre-monarchy days. He built the temple, which was really a royal chapel and which tended to turn Yahweh into the God of the dynasty rather than the God of the people. He established foreign alliances, even through inter-marriage, and this led to the official, government-supported introduction into Israel of the cult of foreign gods. The first two innovations — taxes with forced labor and the new administrative division of the land — led to the split of the nation at Solomon's death: the northern tribes set up their own kingdom (whose rulers, however, followed the example Solomon had set — in setting up, for instance, royal shrines to Yahweh at Bethel and Dan, the southern and northern extremities of their kingdom). The last three innovations bore their most bitter fruits only gradually in the centuries that followed. The official introduction of pagan worship by royal authority took place in the north during the reign of Ahab (874-853 B.C.) and in the south during the reign of Ahaz (736-716 B.C.). With the monarchs themselves introducing paganism, how could the king-controlled cult of Yahweh resist? Social injustice turned into open exploitation of the poor in the north about 750 B.C., and in the south some few decades later. The prophets rose to answer the double threat of pagan cult and social injustice. They fought to save Yahwism from extinction. But they fought to save the kingly ideal too.

When through the influence of his Phoenician wife, Jezebel, Ahab introduced the worship of the Tyrian Baal, the prophet Elijah carried on an almost singlehanded battle against this paganism. That he meant not to innovate but simply to champion the

cause of Moses' God stands out quite clearly from
his journey to Sinai, undertaken in the midst of his
ministry to renew his bond with the God of the covenant (I Kings 19). His battle was long and the
persecution he bore formidable. Calling down a very
lengthy drought on the apostate land, predicting the
early extinction of the paganizing king's dynasty, he
even challenged the prophets of Baal to a public
contest between their gods and his (I Kings
18:20f.). In the presence of a great crowd of
Israelites, he exclaimed, "If Yahweh is God (Elohim), follow Him; if Baal, follow him." When the
contest had proved Baal utterly unable to send
down fire from heaven, but Yahweh powerful
enough to do it, the people cried, "It is Yahweh
who is God!" and slaughtered the Baalist prophets
on the spot. Can these expressions — Elijah's and
the people's — be taken to mean merely that Yahweh is a more powerful deity than Baal, or do they
not rather mean that Yahweh is God while Baal is
not? In its struggle for survival against pagan religion, the practical and implicit monotheism of the
Yahwism of earlier centuries was becoming more
explicit. Later prophets would take up the same
cry, as Yahwism became ever more emphatically —
even belligerently — monotheistic. Over two centuries later, in the southern kingdom, Jeremiah, in
what may have been the inaugural discourse of his
preaching ministry, would complain of Judah's apos-
tasy(Jeremiah 2:11): "Does any nation change its

gods (*elohim*)? and they are not gods at all. But my people have exchanged their glory [Yahweh] for impotence [pagan deities]."

Elijah's successor, the prophet Elisha, averted the threat of total extinction which Yahwism faced under Ahab by encouraging the bloody revolt of Jehu, a devoted Yahwist who annihilated Ahab's line and Baalism from Israel. The new dynasty, of course, encouraged worship of the God of the covenant. This permitted later prophets to concentrate their efforts on the other great evil of the monarchy period: social injustice.

Elijah had vigorously reproved Ahab for high-handed appropriation of private property that did not even stop at murder (I Kings 21). But the blight of social injustice reached its worst only a century later under the prosperity of the rule of Jehu's dynasty. At the news he received of the self-satisfied, formalistic worship of the God of the covenant on the part of northerners — who grew rich by exploiting their fellow Israelites — Amos, though he was a citizen of the southern kingdom and no member of an ecstatic band, felt the divine impulse to undertake the prophetic ministry to recall these ill-enlightened Yahwists to their senses. He traveled north to the shrine of Bethel and there fulminated threats of disaster and destruction against the sinful people. No more than Elijah did he consider himself an innovator. He spoke in Yahweh's name to the people that Yahweh had brought out of

the land of Egypt (Amos 3:1). He recalled the
singular favor that Yahweh had conferred on Israel
in making them His people. True, he did not men-
tion the covenant explicitly, but the reason was his
desire to present the relationship as a favor on Yahweh's part rather than run the risk of having it
understood as a bilateral agreement from which
each of the partners had something to gain: Yahweh, their cult; and they, His protection. He insisted
on Israel's observance of its part of the agreement,
the Decalogue, and vividly underscored the insuffi-
ciency of the externals of cult without righteous living. The prophets have always been credited with
making Yahwism a moral monotheism, that is, of
linking a moral life with worship of an only God —
an exclusive prerogative of Yahwism among the
ancient religions. As we have seen, from the desert
days the Mosaic religion was *practically* monotheistic. So too, in the Decalogue itself the need of
righteous living for the people who would be a
covenant-partner with the righteous Yahweh was
clear. But just as Elijah asserted monotheism with
an unprecedented vehemence, so Amos insisted on
the need for righteousness with such vigor that it
assumed a clarity it had never known before. The
God of Amos is almost starkly a God of righteousness.

Given the perversion of Israel and the clarity of
Amos' conception of Yahweh's righteousness, the
substance of the prophet's message is almost in-

evitable: "The eyes of the Lord Yahweh are upon this sinful kingdom: 'I will destroy it from the face of the earth'" (9:8). He will destroy till hardly a remnant remains (*ibid.*). But this is something new. Despite his unwillingness to innovate, the prophet has asserted something unheard of till then. God will not merely humiliate His faithful people as He did in the period of the Judges; He will destroy them and their kingdom. Even more, along with them will go to destruction their sinful pagan neighbors with whom they had become involved. Yahweh had settled these neighbors in their lands just as He had settled His own people; so too would He send them off into exile. From the days of the patriarchs, and especially from those of Moses, Israel's God had been a God of history — a God directing the history of His people and, ultimately, towards a glorious future. In the brightness of his prophetic penetration Amos perceived Him as Lord of history in an even more absolute sense: He is master of His people's history for extremes of woe as well as for weal, and master of all other peoples too. Heir of the explicit monotheism of Elijah, Amos gave a new insight into Yahweh's *goodness* both in the sense of His beneficence to Israel (since He vigorously emphasized the covenant as a freely given favor) and particularly in the sense of His righteousness. He gave, too, a new insight into Yahweh's *transcendence* as master of the destinies of nations.

A contemporary or close successor of Amos was
Hosea. A northerner, and possibly a member of a
prophetic band, he preached much the same message
as Amos: fidelity to the covenant-God demands a
righteous life; Israel's infidelity, especially their
social injustice, must certainly bring down destruction upon the sinful nation. But Hosea grasped
something about Yahweh that Amos had not seen.
Destruction, indeed, had to come, but it could not
be definitive — not because Israel had grounds for
demanding restoration but because Yahweh could
not have made the covenant merely to bring it to
naught. In a personal tragedy, the gross infidelity of
a wife whom he continued to love, he came to appreciate the attachment of Yahweh to His people.
He drew in great detail what was certainly a shock-
ing picture of the covenant-God as a husband, pas-
sionately in love with Israel, an unfaithful wife — a
wife that must be punished but that ultimately must
also be taken back. He depicted Yahweh struggling
with His own affections (Hosea 11:8f.):

> How can I give you up, O Ephraim [Israel]
>   or hand you over Israel? . . .
> My heart is overcome;
>   my pity blazes out.
> I will not carry out my fierce anger;
>   I will not destroy Ephraim again.
> For I am God and not man,
>   the Holy One in your midst.

The God of Hosea is a God of love.

The destruction foreseen by Amos and Hosea fell upon the northern kingdom in 722 B.C. But the message these men had preached did not perish in the disaster. Committed to writing, it circulated in the surviving kingdom of Judah. There other prophets deepened the insight of these predecessors.

Only a few years after Amos' work at Bethel, Isaiah of Jerusalem received his call to prophesy. The influence of the earlier prophets seems detectable in his outlook and message. Like Amos (and Hosea) he inveighed against formalistic cult and social injustice. Like Amos (and Hosea) he saw Yahweh as a lord of history, directing the course not only of His people's progress but also of their neighbors' — indeed, their very enemies' victories. For him as for Amos, this indicated Yahweh's transcendence. But Isaiah's grasp of the divine transcendence far outstripped his predecessor's. In the very vision in which he received his vocation (Isaiah 6), he saw Yahweh enthroned in awe-inspiring royal majesty, with worshipping seraphim chanting His greatness: "Holy, Holy, Holy." God's "holiness" in Hebrew means His "otherness," His "difference" from creatures, His divine transcendence. Only He is holy and whatever belongs to Him.

Isaiah's God is a God of holiness. But the prophet does not merely directly and vigorously emphasize the divine transcendence (as Amos did less directly and vigorously). He draws a consequence: puny man — in particular, sinful Israel — really has no claims on Yahweh but can only rely on Him and His word. In other words, just as man must be righteous to be a party to a covenant with righteous Yahweh, so weak man must have *faith* in the all-transcending God if he is to enjoy divine help and protection. "Unless you hold fast [to Yahweh] in faith, you will not stand fast," he told the idolatrous King Ahaz (7:9). The notions of faith and trust had been present in the patriarchal accounts. Isaiah made man's faith and divine transcendence correlatives.

A citizen of the Davidic city of Jerusalem, Isaiah also contributed to restoring the kingly ideal. In contrast to the reigning king, the future kings would become once more, like David, Yahweh's instrument for restoring ideal religious and political conditions for the remnant to survive destruction. But we may pass over this point since we are concerned at present with the prophets' conception of God, rather than with the details of His work among His people.

Over a hundred years later when the prophetic movement emerged from more than a half-century of bloody persecution, Zephaniah, Habakkuk and others in Jerusalem developed Isaiah's notion of faith and dependence on the transcendent God. When the fall of the southern kingdom lay only decades away, Zephaniah insisted that salvation would come not to the self-sufficient rebels from Yahwism but only to a humble and lowly remnant who "take refuge in Yahweh's name" (Zephaniah

3:12). When the military power that would pre-
cipitate the destruction was about to make its first
intervention in Judah's affairs, Habakkuk insisted
that only the righteous man would survive the
destruction "because of his faith" (Habakkuk 2:4).

It was at this time — and even shortly before —
that Jeremiah and the preachers of the Deuterono-
mic reform were exploiting the potentialities of
Hosea's message. The Sinai covenant had been a
totally gratuitous favor given the people by Yahweh, not for any profit that He hoped to gain from
them but simply because He loved the patriarchs
and chose their descendants. Yahweh's great love
for His people demanded a wholehearted, even pas-
sionate, attachment to Him. Emphasis on a religion
of the heart led Jeremiah to proclaim the period that
would follow the destruction as a time for a new
covenant, in which not simply the people as a whole
would be bound to Yahweh but each person among
them would "know" Him — that is, not merely
acknowledge Him as God but enjoy His intimacy.
Thus the notion of Yahweh as a God and a judge of
individual men, not merely of a people, made its
appearance.

In 587 B.C. Jerusalem fell, and the Israelite monarchy became forever a thing of the past. By that
time the prophets had explicitly formulated in quite
unambiguous terms the absolute oneness of a personal God in opposition to pagan polytheism: His
utter transcendence, as shown in His lordship of

history and in His demanding faith and trust on the part of man; His complete righteousness, demanding righteousness in those who would enjoy partnership with Him and destroying those who refused to be righteous; and His great goodness — greater, in a sense, even than His righteousness — showing itself not only in the gratuitous favor which was the covenant He made with His people but also in the personal intimacy with Himself which He would grant the survivors of the exile.

THE EXILIC AND POSTEXILIC PERIODS

The Exile was a time of captivity in a foreign land, the postexilic period an era of dependence in Palestine on foreign rulers. Our knowledge of these centuries is piecemeal. But the Bible, the archeologist and the historian furnish us enough information to assess Israel's growth in her appreciation of God during these centuries. The captive people arriving in Mesopotamia found the prophet Ezekiel at work insisting on the utter transcendence of the lord of history as Amos and Isaiah had done, and proclaiming the absolute certainty of restoration since Yahweh had decreed it. When the time drew near for their return to Palestine, the great anonymous prophet called Second Isaiah announced to them, in a style reminiscent of Deuteronomy and Jeremiah, that the time for the new and gratuitous covenant of the good God was at hand. When they had settled down in and around Jerusalem, the prophets Haggai

and Zechariah helped them to reorganize and re-
build, and reanimated their hope in the designs of
Yahweh for their future. But then the prophetic
charism failed. Two or three isolated voices delivered brief prophetic oracles during the centuries
that followed (Malachi, Obadiah, Joel), and prophets were no more.

In the name of Israel's Persian overlords, the
priest Ezra proclaimed as law of the land the written
Torah (law) of Moses — the substance of our Old
Testament Pentateuch which had been assembled
into a whole during the Exile. There thus began for
the remnant of the people that had returned a long
period of quiet life under foreign rule, with the
books of Moses and the writings of the past prophets
for them to meditate upon. In this way Israel became the "people of the Book," and Judaism was
born.

The setting down in writing — whether of the
Law or of the prophets — and above all the proclamation of the Torah as the law of the land tended to
retard further change or development. But in the
five centuries that followed, change and development there were, even as regards Israel's appreciation of God.

When the Law and the prophets' writings were
being assembled in captivity, Israelite monotheism
had reached its extreme development. Second Isaiah
had filled his message with explicit and emphatic
declarations of monotheism. He had presented

Yahweh exclaiming, "I am first and I am last; apart from me there is no God" (Isaiah 44:6). He had depicted Israel's God pronouncing Himself God of the Gentiles too: "Apart from me there is no God; . . . turn to me and find salvation, all you ends of the earth, for I am God, and there is no other" (Isaiah 45:21f.). He had ridiculed the helplessness of Babylonia's gods (Isaiah 46). Later writers would produce biting satires on the folly of pagan idolatry. The author of the Wisdom of Solomon, for example, would mock (chapter 13): "How vain are all men who have not known God . . . but have considered as gods fire or wind or air or the starry vault of heaven or the stormy sea or the lights of heaven. . . . But how [much more] miserable are they — and their hopes set on dead things — who have called gods the work of human hands." The mockery continues with a sarcastic description of the idol-maker's labor on motionless, senseless wood and of his idolatrous prayer: "He is not ashamed to pray to a lifeless thing — to ask weakness for health, a dead thing for life, very impotence for help, something motionless for aid on a journey, and something with utterly feeble hands for gain . . . and success. . . ."

In exile, too, Israel's sense of the divine transcendence had reached full development, as also her sense of divine goodness. Second Isaiah had proclaimed Yahweh the only omnipotent creator and master of history (for example, Isaiah 45). Later writers would depict Yahweh's future interventions in history on a more cosmic scale and expect them to have world-wide and definitive results. The author of the book of Daniel (chapter 7) would see the one God pronouncing sentence on world empire after world empire till He established the rule of the holy people of the Most High, whose "kingdom shall be an everlasting kingdom and all empires will serve and obey" it (v. 27). The all-transcending God would intervene definitively on behalf of His own.

Israel's sense of the guilt and sin that had led to the downfall of the monarchy had grown during exile. This increased the people's sense of the distance between themselves and God. The mounting importance attached to the written Law tended to push God still higher into His heaven. However, the Torah expressed His will for His people's good. In fact, it was His wisdom come down among them. But it *did* stand between Him and them. So overwhelming did their sense of His greatness become that they no longer pronounced His proper name. Instead of "Yahweh" He was simply "the Lord." Yet, so certain were they that He would right all the wrongs they suffered that they became convinced that the righteous who had known only suffering their whole life through must rise from the dead to receive their reward (Dan. 12), or must after death become like the angels and dwell with God (Wisd. 3-5). Their heartfelt attachment to the

good God of their fathers led them even regularly to
address Him in prayers as "our King, our Father."
Thus, throughout the last pre-Christian centuries the
Jewish sense of the *utter transcendence* and bound-
less *goodness* of the *only* God grew ever deeper and
fuller.

GOD IN THE NEW TESTAMENT: GOD'S SELF-REVELATION IN CHRIST

Sometime after the year 25 a young Jewish teach-
er began going about the Palestinian countryside
preaching to the crowds. He came from the little
Galilean town of Nazareth, and His name was
Jesus. He gathered a small group of especially close
disciples about Him, to whom He gave more and
more attention as His popularity began to wane.
Clashes with the Jewish authorities, after just a few
short years of preaching led to His condemnation as
a blasphemer against the God of the covenant and
a rebel against the Roman authorities. He was exe-
cuted by crucifixion. Shortly afterwards His closest
disciples began to preach that He had risen from the
dead, and none of the adversaries could satisfac-
torily explain away His empty tomb. His followers
proclaimed that all the designs which the God of
the covenant had on His people either had been or
would be realized in the risen Jesus; and they found,
first, thousands of Jews, and then numberless pagans, ready to accept their claims. The movement
spread. The original little band together with a few

other early Christian leaders organized the ever greater numbers of believers into communities awaiting the final and definitive return of Christ.

Our knowledge of these events comes mainly from the writings we call the New Testament; however other writings contemporary with or hardly later than the New Testament books furnish quite ample confirmation of them. In the New Testament the gospels contain the memories of the teachings and doings of Jesus preserved by the very first Christian generation, while the epistles contain instructions to various first-century Christian communities from the Apostles who were organizing them. In the former we can find what Jesus had to say about God; in the latter, the Apostolic teaching.

We need hardly point out that the New Testament simply takes the Old Testament idea of God for granted. This is true particularly, though not exclusively, of Jesus' teaching in the gospels. Affirmations of God's oneness, His transcendence or His righteousness, when they occur, serve as evident principles from which to draw conclusions and, in themselves, need no proof. For example, when St. Paul in Romans 1:18ff. argues against the folly of the pagans' polytheism, he is not trying to establish monotheism but to illustrate the great need the Gentiles have of redemption, despite their futile religiosity and their proud claims to wisdom.

What Jesus said about God, especially to His disciples, must have sounded very familiar. He told of the God who had spoken to and through Moses and the prophets. He told of the God, the coming of whose kingdom or reign the Jews were awaiting. He also spoke of the God who showed a loving and paternal providence for His own. But there were differences too — differences which may go unperceived by the hasty reader but which are quite profound.

Jesus never calls God "the Lord" (Yahweh) except when He quotes an Old Testament passage containing the expression. Either He uses the general term "God" (in the Greek of the New Testament *theos,* or in the Hebrew *elohim*) or the title "Father." This latter term, applied to God very rarely in the Old Testament (about a dozen times), occurs over 250 times in the New, and many of these instances occur in the gospels. In fact, we may consider "Father" the New Testament name for God, or Jesus' name for Him, as Yahweh was the divine title employed by Moses.

Another remarkable point: Jesus never presents God as Father of the people of His covenant (as the Old Testament and the rabbis did), much less as the Father of all men. He is Jesus' own Father and Father to Jesus' disciples. Anyone may become a disciple, of course — and all are invited to discipleship — but only the one who *has* become Jesus' follower finds Jesus referring to God as "your Father." Jesus' relationship to Him is unique — so much so that in reference to one another God and

Jesus can be called quite simply "*the* Father" and "*the* Son." The disciples' relationship to the Father seems to be a share in Jesus' own. "My Father," He says in Matthew 11:27 — the "Lord of heaven and earth" according to v. 25 — "has given everything over to me; no one knows the Son [Jesus] except the Father, and no one knows the Father except the Son and the one to whom the Son chooses to reveal Him."

A third notable innovation: divine fatherhood does not refer simply to God's paternal providence for Jesus and His disciples. It does, of course, include this. Jesus could insist (Matt. 6:25ff.) that the disciples learn a lesson of carefree reliance on God from the birds and wild flowers, which He clothes and feeds: "Are you not of much more value than they? . . . Your heavenly Father knows that you need" food and clothing. But divine paternity implies much more: God's sons must imitate their Father, and this means living a life of love. "Love," Jesus demands (Lk. 6:27ff.), even "your enemies, do good to those who hate you, bless those who curse you, pray for those who calumniate you, . . . and [thus] you will be sons of the Most High, for He is kindly to the ingrates and wicked. You must be compassionate as your Father is compassionate." And since Jesus is God's Son in a much more complete way than the disciples, they can then best imitate God by imitating Him: "A disciple is not above his master; every perfect disciple will be like his master" (Lk. 6:40). "Whoever among you should wish to be first must be your servant just as the Son of Man came not to be served but to serve and to give His life as a means to set the many free" (Matt. 20:27f.).

From the days of Sinai it was necessary for the Israelites to be righteous because their God was righteous; otherwise, they could not be partners to His covenant. Perhaps some Israelites had conceived of this righteousness as an imitation of Yahweh's. Certainly many of the later rabbis did. They did this sparingly, however, and even then in ways quite foreign to the gospels. For example, God supplied a model for burying the dead because, according to Deuteronomy 34, Yahweh provided for Moses' burial. Or again, for afflicting the wicked! In Sirach 12 the aging Jerusalem sage who composed the book counseled the withholding of alms from the wicked since "even the Most High hates sinners and will take vengeance on the impious"! Jesus, on the other hand, held up only God's beneficence — or, more precisely, His *love* — for imitation, and He connected the duty of imitating God with the disciples' sonship.

He connected the duty of imitating God with the disciples' sonship. Like father like son. We would be tempted to conclude: God's paternity must be more than a metaphor. There must be a real communication of life from God to the disciple that founds the disciple's duty of resembling His divine

Father, in the same way as physical generation causes the resemblance of children to their parents. But the Synoptic Gospels do not go so far — at least explicitly. Continuing our reasoning in view of the fact that Jesus enjoys an altogether unique sonship and, in addition to Himself, only His disciples may call God "Father," we would be tempted to conclude: their sonship is simply a share in His, and He is the great imitator of God whom they must resemble if they are to be like the Father. This, too, is not explicitly affirmed in the Synoptic Gospels. However, it seems evidently implied by them. The Johannine writings and the New Testament epistles had no difficulty whatever in unhesitatingly affirming these points. But we shall examine them later.

Jesus held up only God's love as model. In fact, love was practically the only divine attribute He emphasized. True, nowhere in the Synoptic Gospels does Jesus speak of God's "love" explicitly except in that portion of the Sermon on the Mount cited above, where the disciples must imitate God's manner of acting by "loving" their enemies. But His insistence that He had been sent by God to call sinners to repentance; His behavior as God's legate, as "friend of publicans and sinners" and benefactor of the physically ailing and spiritually uninstructed; His demands in God's name for mercy, compassion, and kindness — all sufficed for the Apostle Peter to sum up His entire public ministry sometime after the Resurrection in these words, "He went about doing good and healing all who were oppressed by the devil" (Acts 10:38), and they surely suffice for us to sum up His message as a proclamation of overwhelming divine benevolence. The other New Testament writings will unhesitatingly and consistently call this divine benevolence love. Jesus, of course, does not deny eschatological punishment (late pre-Christian Judaism believed in punishment beyond the grave as well as in a reward for the righteous), but He simply reserves it for those who refuse to accept God's love.

Before we move on to a consideration of the other New Testament writings, we must spend at least a few moments examining what Jesus said about His own identity and about the Holy Spirit. The substance of His affirmations about His own person we have already seen; He is God's Son in an altogether unique sense, enjoying an intimacy with the Father which no one can share unless He Himself grants it. A breathtaking claim! We might even say: a claim to divinity!

Nowhere in the Synoptic Gospels, of course, does Jesus describe Himself as God (*theos*). Had He done so during His brief ministry, His monotheistic Jewish audience would certainly have understood Him either to be claiming pure and simple identity with the covenant God from whom, however, He distinguished Himself by regularly calling Him His Father — or to be identifying Himself as a second deity distinct from, though in harmony with, Yahweh, in other words, either unmodified Old Testament monotheism or pagan polytheism. Hence, Jesus avoided the term.

In fact, He accepted and confirmed the emphatic monotheism of His fellow Jews. He claimed for Himself total harmony with, or rather dependence upon, the Father. He was the Father's legate (Mk. 12:6) with the Father's message to proclaim (Lk. 4:17 ff). He always obeyed and did what pleased the Father (Jn. 5:38; 8:29; cf. Mk. 14:36). But He also claimed an unheard-of intimacy with God. He alone knew the Father well enough to reveal Him to men (Matt. 11:27). In fact, so exclusively was the Father revealing Himself through Jesus that to accept Jesus was to accept the Father (Mk. 9:37), and to reject Him meant to reject the Father.

In addition to these explicit claims of all-but-identity with God, Jesus also made what we might call implicit claims in the way He worked wonders and the demands He made on disciples. The New Testament accounts of His wonder-working show Him performing miracles in a way quite different from those recorded in any Old Testament (or pagan) miracle stories. Most often He quite simply and directly gave orders to the natural forces or diseases or devils without any request for divine help whatever, and they complied. As regards the demands He made on His disciples, He expected them to be completely devoted to Him — so completely that anyone who loved father, mother, wife, children, brothers, sisters, or even his very life more than Jesus could not be a disciple (Lk. 14:26; cf. Matt. 10:37). He declared that He would judge "all the nations" and determine whether they would enter the kingdom prepared for the blessed of His Father or "the enduring fire prepared for the devil and his angels" on the basis of their attitude towards Him (Matt. 25:31-46). It is then not surprising that, although during His brief years of preaching neither He nor His contemporaries explicitly called Jesus "God," He came to be called "the Lord" shortly after His Resurrection — in the same sense in which Judaism used the term of the God of Israel — and sometime thereafter, quite simply "God."

The "Spirit of God" for Old Testament authors meant a divine force. They employed the term of violent winds, of violent movements of human anger, and of a variety of other manifestations of power — all of these, of course, acting under the control of God's providence. Then, too, it was a "divine" or "holy" spirit which assisted the Israelite heroes during the time of the Judges in their efforts to deliver their people from oppression. So, too, did a holy spirit come down upon the prophets and provide them with the oracles they delivered in Yahweh's name. During the exilic and postexilic periods prophets told the people that when the time of God's great future intervention in their history came, He would pour out His spirit not simply on their leaders but on all the people, not merely in a temporary manner but permanently. Accordingly, John the Baptist told the crowds that the one who was coming after him would immerse or, to use the Greek word, "baptize" them in *a* or *the* "holy spirit" (Mk. 1:8). Jesus Himself was full of this Spirit and assured His disciples that the Spirit would aid and support them in persecution, even instructing them how to answer their persecutors (Mk. 1:10; Lk. 4:1; 12:12). This teaching role of the Spirit makes us think of a person rather than simply a power. In the Fourth Gospel, Jesus' words about the Spirit at the supper table leave no doubt about His personality; He bears witness, convicts the unbelieving world, dwells with and is in the disciples, teaching them "all the truth" (Jn. 15:26-16:15; cf. 14:15-17). He is even called the "Paraclete" ("advocate" or "consoler"). But how clearly Jesus' hearers understood that the Spirit they hoped to receive was a person is difficult to say. They may well not have grasped His personality at all.

Full appreciation of the Father, the God whom Jesus revealed, of Jesus Himself, and of the Spirit came only with the Passion and Resurrection of Jesus along with the following outpouring of the Spirit upon the early Church. Jesus' predictions of His sufferings during His public ministry had only brought consternation upon the Apostles. When they saw Him triumphant over death and com-

pletely and definitively beyond the reach of the
woes and misfortunes of ordinary human existence,
they recognized Him as "the Lord." As they announced the good news of salvation achieved by
the risen Jesus, they gradually realized why He had
had to suffer and so enter into His glory. He had
passed from this life by an act of total self-renuncia-
tion, so that we might be able to make the passage
with Him. His life and, above all, His Passion and
Resurrection were the revelation of the extremes
to which the Father's good will towards men would
go — the revelation of God as love. As the Apostles
saw the work of the Spirit in the infant Church, they
began to realize quite clearly that He was a person
and to understand what His proper relation was to
Father and Son. In their letters to various Christian
communities they explained these things. In the
Fourth Gospel, composed towards the end of the
first century, this full understanding of the mystery
of Jesus was recorded in gospel form. A brief
glance at these writings — epistles and Johannine
gospel — will show how the Apostles expressed this
full appreciation.

St. Paul wrote, for example, to the Romans that
"God proves his love for us in that Christ died for
us while we were still sinners" (5:8), reconciling
us to God and giving us assurance of full salvation
(final resurrection), since we already possess a
share in His risen life (5:10; cf. 8:10 f.). Of course,
it is through sharing in His sufferings and renuncia-

tion that we share in His glory (8:17). Therefore, no tribulations, however great, "can separate us from the love of God in Christ Jesus our Lord," but in and by them we win the victory because of Him who has loved us (8:35-39). He wrote too that God's gift to us of His Spirit is the manifestation of His great love for us: "God's love has been poured into our hearts by the Holy Spirit who has been given us" (5:5) — the Spirit that makes us sons of God, "for whoever are led about by the Spirit of God are sons of God" (8:14). We are sons, "predestined to reproduce the image of His Son" (8:29) because we have the Spirit of Christ and are, therefore, one with Christ (8:9 f., 16).

What he wrote to the Christians of Rome does not differ from what he wrote less diffusely to the church in Galatia: "When the appointed time came God sent his Son . . . that we might receive adoption as sons. And the proof that you are sons? God has sent the Spirit of his Son into our hearts crying out, 'Abba, Father' " (4:4-7). Our possession of the Spirit enables us to share in the Son's filial relationship to the divine Father. But we have received the Spirit through our faith in Christ (3:2), the "Son of God who loved [us] and delivered himself up for" us (2:20). By faith we have accepted the revelation of God's great love in Christ. No wonder that the Spirit we have received with this faith should inspire us to live by love (5:13, 22). No wonder that for the Christian "neither circumcision has any importance nor the lack of it, but faith expressing itself through love" (5:6). We may even add that the Christian's love simply reflects and imitates Christ's (and therefore God's) own love shown in the Cross. The epistle to the Ephesians (5:1 f.) urges: "Be imitators of God like dearly loved children and walk in love." God has loved us and, therefore, made us His children. Our duty as children is to imitate Him or, rather, to imitate the very love by which He made us children. And this means what? It means to "walk in love even as Christ loved you and delivered Himself up for us."

In Jesus — who incidentally is also God (Rom. 9:5[?]; Tit. 2:13) — we have come to know God as loving, as Father. By accepting Jesus through faith we received His Spirit, and the Spirit makes us one with Him and so enables us to share the Father's life in and with Jesus — life that expresses itself in love.

St. John wrote practically the same thing. "In the beginning the Word [God's effective self-revelation — see Jn. 1:18] existed" already. "This Word was with God." Indeed, "this Word was God," that is, was divine (Jn. 1:1). Finally, "the Word became flesh," that is, weak man — the man who was Jesus (1:14) — so that He might give "to as many as received Him — [that is,] who believed in His name — the power to become children of God" (1:12). Or a little later (3:14-16): "God so loved the world that he gave [in the Passion and Resurrection] His only-begotten Son that everyone who believes in him may not be lost but may enjoy possession of enduring life," that is, "may in him possess" this life everlasting. The Father made a unique communication to the Son before the world's creation, and the gift was His love (17:24); this love Jesus has come (and died and risen) to communicate to the disciples (17:26) who have accepted Him by faith (17:6 ff.). Possessed of the Spirit after and as a result of Jesus' Passion-Resurrection (16:7ff.; cf. 14:16f.) — the Spirit who, coming from and sent by Father and Son, keeps them united with Christ (16:13-15) — they must live a life of love like Jesus' (15:9-17).

Finally, in his first epistle John explains, "God is love. God's love has become manifest to us in that God has sent his only-begotten Son into the world so that we might live through him," sharing His life; He "has sent him as a propitiation for our sins" (4:8-10). By faith, the work of God's Spirit within us (4:2-13), we have accepted Jesus as the Son of God sent by the Father as Savior of the world (4:14 f.) or, in other words, we "have come to know and believe the love which God has for us" (4:16). Since God is love and by faith we have accepted Him as such, then we must lead lives of love: "Let us love one another, for love is from God, and everyone who loves has been born of God and knows God; the man who does not love has not known God because God is love" (4:7 f.). "The man who dwells in love dwells in God and God dwells in him" (4:16).

The New Testament, then, underscores — or, rather, develops — two interdependent, if not identical, aspects of God: He is love, He is Father. He wills to be our Father if we accept union with Jesus His Son by possession of Their Spirit, and so begin to lead the divine life of love.

We may now sum up the biblical conception of God in a few brief remarks. Israel's conception of divinity differed from that of the pagans since the very days of the patriarchs. As far as we can tell, only one superior Power claimed the cult of the people's ancestors, a God whom they had come to know through His revelation of His designs for good on their future history. In the Mosaic period Israel came to know Him as Yahweh, the personal God of the Sinai covenant, intolerant of His covenant-people's worship of any other deity — righteous as they had bound themselves to be by the terms of the covenant — and by the covenant generously making Himself master of their future for their good. At the gradual collapse of Israelite society under the monarchy, the result of pagan inroads and formalistic Yahwism, the prophets came first to appreciate fully, and then proclaimed to the people the sole and all-transcendent Lord of all history for woe as well as for weal, a Lord righteous even to the point of repudiating the covenant with a sinful people, but good to the point of bringing them back to Himself despite all their wickedness. In the postexilic period Judaism simply continued in possession of this conception of God, though broadening and deepening it somewhat. It should be noted that none of this Israelite idea of God was the result of abstract speculation about divinity (as were the Greek ideas). Israel knew God even in patriarchal times from His self-revelation, His breaking into and changing the course of their history. The gradual development of their knowledge of Him came from further divine self-revelation in God's repeated interventions in or management of their history. In short, the people of Israel knew God from what He had done in or made of their history. The Old Testament is the record of this divine self-revelation. God's last great historical intervention, in which He completed His self-revelation, was the Christ-event: the life, Passion, and Resurrection of Jesus.

The New Testament takes for granted the conception of God which Judaism possessed at the end of the Old Testament, but deepens and broadens it immensely. Jesus presented Himself as revealer of God to men. In the light not only of what He said, but especially of what He did (His Passion-Resurrection, in particular), the New Testament authors set down this revelation. God is not merely the sole, all-transcendent Deity, who is also blamelessly righteous and wonderfully beneficent. But His beneficence blazes out with such over-whelming brilliance in the life, death, and Resurrection of Jesus that no other word than "love" can serve to designate it. St. John can write quite simply, "God is love," since all that we have seen or know of God through and in Jesus is love. But Jesus Himself does not use this term. Rather He declares — and, of course, the New Testament authors echo Him — that God is Father, a Father in the very real sense that He has an only-begotten Son. He wants to be Father to men as He is to Jesus, and will become such if they accept union with His Son by possession of the Son's (and the Father's) Holy Spirit. But this vital union, which men sealed with the Spirit enjoy with the Father in and through the crucified-risen Jesus, expresses itself in their lives of love, a universal, generously self-sacrificing benevolence such as no one had ever preached before. It would be the task of the Church and her theologians to work out a technical terminology to express the mutual relations of Father, Son, and Spirit (one nature, three persons, Holy Trinity) and the relations of Christians to them (participation in divine life, grace, virtues . . .).

THE BIBLE: RECORD OF GOD'S SELF-REVELATION TO MEN

The Bible is a collection of disparate writings composed in various places, scattered about the eastern half of the Mediterranean Sea, during a period lasting perhaps a millennium. It may be that the only thing the authors all shared was their acceptance of the God of Israel and, for New Testament writers, the God of Jesus.

If we examine the books we call the Old Testament, we find that for the most part they are historical, either in the sense that they narrate past events or in the sense that they assess contemporary events (the prophets). It is generally agreed that the narrative books which treat of the earlier centuries of Israel's history existed originally in oral form. Traditions about the patriarchal wanderings or the making of the Sinai Covenant were recited or chanted at the various Yahwist shrines in the Promised Land, and stories about the later champions of the people were told for generations around Israelite campfires. All recounted the great things that Israel's God had accomplished for His people. Gradually written down and gathered into various collections, they finally appeared in the editions we have of the earlier Old Testament books (Genesis, Exodus, Numbers, Joshua, Judges). When later authors wished to compose accounts of the monarchy period as a sequel to these earlier histories, they had written records they could utilize — chronicles, for example — as well as traditions. Carefully, they worked this material over, sifting their sources for the data they wanted, discarding the rest. All of the Old Testament books treating of pre-exilic times were composed in Hebrew by Israelites either in Israel or during exile in Mesopotamia.

All of them recount Israel's history, which is simply the story of Israel's relationship to Yahweh or, since God revealed Himself in this history, the story of God's self-revelation to Israel in history.

The great prophets, at least some of them, had not only preached but also set their oracles down in writing. They — or more likely their disciples — collected and edited their preaching, often supplying narrative about the prophet's life and ministry or circumstantial background for this or that oracle. Since the prophets' great struggle was to make the people recognize and understand the God who was at work in their history, their books, too, told part of the story of the self-revelation in history of Israel's God.

After the Torah had become the law of the land, when the histories of pre-exilic times had been published and the works of most of the great prophets had begun to circulate, a rather motley assortment of literary compositions started to appear. For example, there were stories like Ruth illustrating the generosity of the covenant God to those who proved faithful to Him. There were collections like Proverbs teaching how to live the good life under the Covenant. There were poetic discussions of great unanswered questions, like Job's question about the unmerited sufferings of the faithful servants of Israel's God. Finally, there was the collection of prayers to the covenant God used in the Temple worship. Though, strictly speaking, they do not re-

count the history of God's relation to Israel, these
writings do illumine various aspects of this relationship, written, as all of them were, within the covenant framework.

The Torah or written Law of Moses, Israel's
great mediator with God, had been normative for
Jewish life since Ezra's time.[9] Given the extraordinary role of the great prophets in Israel's history,
their writings naturally enjoyed a similar authority.
That the great series of histories of pre-exilic Israel,
which we have in Joshua-II Kings, should have
gained a comparable position of respect may have
been due to any of several reasons. The group responsible for the Book of Deuteronomy as we now
have it was also responsible for them: acceptance
of Deuteronomy as authoritative may have prepared for acceptance of these histories. They stand
in such close relation to the prophetic books, supplying a background to these latter, that acceptance
of the prophetic literature may have aided acceptance of them. In fact, they came to be called the
"Earlier Prophets" and the prophetic books proper
the "Later Prophets." Or, finally, they contain so
many of the stories of Israel's earlier heroes (as
these accounts had been handed down for cen-

---

[9] There is some disagreement about the precise date at which
the Torah became normative for Jewish life. If it was not accepted
universally in the time of Ezra, at the very latest it was accepted
by the year 300 B.C. (since the Samaritan Pentateuch — a Hebrew
version of the "five books of Moses" accepted by the schismatic
Samaritans — and the Septuagint [Greek] translation of the Bible's
first five books date from shortly after 300 B.C.).

turies) that the very sacredness of the stories they contained may well have conveyed authority on these editions of them. Thus, "The Law and the Prophets (Earlier and Later)" — the great story (though interpolated with laws and interpretation) of Israel's history from patriarchal times till the postexilic period — came to be the great Book in the light of which the people lived when prophetism became extinct; and whatever other writings may have survived from earlier times fell into oblivion.[10]

But as the Old Testament period moved to its close, literature on various aspects of the covenant-relationship between God and Israel proliferated. Much, if not most, of it pretended to be the work of authoritative older figures — prophets, for example, or even Moses himself. Other compositions appeared as the work of sages, that group of thinkers who, especially after the disappearance of prophetism, tried to guide the people by their counsels as the prophets had by their oracles. It is difficult to say by what criterion certain of these later "Writings," as they were called, came to be accepted as an authoritative appendix to the Law and the Prophets in Palestinian Judaism. Perhaps because the collection of the books of "Moses and the Prophets" was considered complete, reception

---

10 "The Law and the Prophets" are mentioned in Sirach 48:22 and Isaiah, Jeremiah, Ezekiel, and the Twelve (that is, the minor prophets) are mentioned in Sirach 49:12. Since this book was written shortly after 200 B.C., these two parts of the Old Testament were accepted by that year at the latest.

of writings that claimed Mosaic or prophetic origin was precluded. For the rest, it was mainly works of sages that found acceptance.[11]

The Greek-speaking Jews of Alexandria, however, seem to have been somewhat less stringent in their reception of the more recent writings. They accepted not only more compositions of sages than their coreligionists in Palestine (Wisdom, Sirach), but also fuller Greek editions of Hebrew books,[12] two additional stories of pre-exilic and exilic times like Esther and Ruth (Tobit, Judith), and even two detailed accounts of Judaism's heroic struggle for survival in the second pre-Christian century (I-II Maccabees). Several of these writings had been composed in Greek, though many were translations from Hebrew or Aramaic originals never accepted by Palestinian Jewry. We have no indication that all Judaism, whether in Palestine or in the Dispersion, agreed about the precise content of the "Writings" appended to "the Law and the Prophets" until as late as the end of the first Christian century or thereabouts. By that time Rome had destroyed Jerusalem, and Christians had exploited Old Testament writings — especially as they existed

11 There were at least some "Writings" accepted as authoritative before the year 132 B.C. The preface to the Greek translation of Sirach mentions them, and it dates from about that year. These "Writings" include Psalms, Proverbs, Qoheleth (Ecclesiastes), the Canticle of Canticles, Job, Daniel, Ruth, Esther, and the work of the Chronicler (Ezra-Nehemiah and I-II Chronicles).

12 The Greek Old Testament also contains fuller (that is, more lengthy) editions of Esther and Daniel and also of Jeremiah if we consider the Book of Baruch an addition to the Book of Jeremiah.

in Greek translation — for apologetic purposes.
Against that background a Jewish council held
about 100 A.D. at Jamnia, a few miles south of
Jaffa and west of Jerusalem, decided which books
would thenceforth be regarded as normative or
"canonical."[13]

Christians, however, continued to use many of
the writings that Greek-speaking Jews had formerly
held in veneration — books usually called "deutero-
canonical" since they do appear in the Christian but
not at all in the Jewish canon.[14]

After the Holy Spirit's coming upon the Church,
the early Christian preachers began to proclaim to
Jew and to Gentile the "good news" or "gospel" (in
Greek, *euangelion*) of God's full self-revelation to
men in the Christ-event (that is, the public ministry,
Passion, and Resurrection of Jesus of Nazareth)
and to explain it in more detail to those who accepted their message. In all likelihood, early written
notes helped the first preachers to remember both
the chief points of their proclamation (in Greek,
kerygma) and the details of further explanation (in
Greek, *didache,* or teaching). St. Paul in particular,
but others too, sent written explanations on specific points to communities they had founded or to
which they felt especially obligated (and at times

[13] By 130 A.D. the books of this Jewish canon had been re-
translated into Greek by Aquila. — The use of the term "canonical"
in this sense dates only from the fourth century.

[14] At the time of the Protestant Reformation, the Reformers rejected the Greek (Christian) canon and adopted the Jewish canon
as their official list of Old Testament books.

to individuals too) but which they could not visit when the need for such explanations arose. Naturally this written teaching of Christ's Apostles was treasured by those who received it. Finally, four serious and thorough attempts were made to organize the bulk of the traditional explanations of the good news of Christ in orderly fashion on the pattern of the basic proclamation. Called "gospels" and produced by men or by groups closely associated with the Apostles, they replaced the earlier notes that preachers must have used. It is not surprising that these epistles and gospels containing the Apostolic proclamation and explanation of the final great intervention of God in man's history, became as normative for the early Christian community as "the Law and Prophets" had become for Judaism. Since one of the gospels (St. Luke's) had a companion volume ("The Acts of the Apostles," or, more precisely, "Acts of Apostles") showing the fulfilment of Jesus' work in the early ministry of certain Apostles, this latter book won acceptance too.

Before the end of the Apostolic Age the first persecutions had broken out. The era of epistle-writing was not yet over, and problems arising for persecuted communities could be met by this means. But the Apostle John or someone close to him chose to meet it by a means which persecuted Judaism had used: an apocalypse. In a series of visions describing the present sufferings and the future glory of the

Church, he exhorted suffering Christians to perseverance. As Apostolic teaching and, therefore, as an instructional though symbolic treatment of the full and final consummation of the Christ-event, it too received full acceptance.

Of course, it took some time — well into the second century — for the majority of the various Christian communities, spread over the Roman Empire and even beyond its frontiers, to come to know of Apostolic writings sent to individual communities or persons. By that time it was not always easy to distinguish between these original writings and the later compositions which pretended to be the work of Apostles. Hence, particular communities often hesitated over certain writings. By the third century the bulk of New Testament writings (the four gospels and most of the epistles) were accepted universally and were already called "the Books of the New Testament" — that is, of the new covenant or relationship of God and men in Christ — as opposed to the Jewish "Books of the Old Testament."[15] By the fourth century complete and official lists or "canons" of the apostolic books began to be published in various places.[16]

This extremely brief survey illustrates two points about the various Old Testament and New Testament books accepted by Judaism and Christianity.

---

[15] See A. Wikenhauser, *New Testament Introduction* (New York: Herder, 1958), p. 32.

[16] For a more detailed discussion of the history of the New Testament canon see A. Wikenhauser, *op. cit.*, pp. 18-61.

First, they are for the most part historical in the sense that they either directly recount or at least illumine God's revelation of Himself in the course of Israel's history and in the Christ-event. Secondly, the criterion used by late Judaism and early Christianity to determine which writings should serve as authentic norms for Synagogue and Church seems to have been the official character of their authors — Moses, the Prophets and the sages for the Old Testament Books, and the Apostles for the New. It was not maintained that the actual writing or dictating was necessarily done by these authorities, but that their teaching or preaching had been incorporated into the books. Thus, the early Church considered the Gospels of Mark and Luke as Apostolic preaching because these men, though not Apostles, were close disciples of Peter and Paul respectively. We have, then, in the Bible an official account of God's self-revelation to men produced by official witnesses or proclaimers of that divine self-revelation.

But to understand fully the esteem the biblical writings enjoyed, we must recall that the Old Testament prophets — and Moses was considered the greatest of them (Deut. 34:10-12) — were not merely God's officially commissioned messengers; they were also especially illumined for understanding the divine message and had been extraordinarily assisted in announcing it.

Because wisdom, at least in the later Old Testament period, was conceived of as God's own wisdom come to dwell among men in the form of the Mosaic Law (Sir. 24), it is not surprising that the sages were also regarded as peculiarly endowed, all the more since they and their counsel-giving — at least in some sense — took the place of the prophets when these latter disappeared (cf. Wisd. 7-9 or Sir. 51:13 ff.). The Apostles too, of course, were not only official preachers but were especially aided by the Holy Spirit in their role as the prophets had been in theirs. Hence, the biblical writings from the very start were considered not merely official accounts by official witnesses but accounts by witnesses extraordinarily assisted in their composition. It is small wonder that these writings came not only to be cited as normative for Jewish or Christian life but as sacred and inspired. For example, II Timothy 3:15 f. speaks of the "Sacred Letters" or Scriptures "inspired by God" capable of instructing in salvation through faith in Christ Jesus. Even earlier in the gospels and in the Acts Jesus Himself and the Apostles referred to the Old Testament writings as composed by men "through whom the Holy Spirit" was speaking (for example, Matt. 22:43; Acts 1:16).

As Christian teachers repeatedly referred to this character of the biblical writings, they relied on the expressions just listed as well as a number of others, either found in the Bible or invented by themselves.

For example, they called the entire Bible what the prophets had called individual oracles: the word of God (cf. Matt. 15:6; Jn. 1:35). From this notion and that of the Holy Spirit's speaking "through" someone, it was just a step to calling God the "author" of the Bible or to treating the human writers as the "instruments" He had used to compose it. These two became the terms Christian theologians and even Church authorities exploited in speaking of the unique divine intervention responsible for the production of the Old and New Testaments. Thus the First Vatican Council declared that the Church regards the biblical writings as sacred and canonical, because "written under the inspiration of the Holy Spirit they have God as *author*" (*Enchiridion Biblicum* 77 [62], italics added). Pope Leo XIII, referring to this declaration of the Council in his encyclical on Scripture studies, *Providentissimus Deus,* understood it to mean that "the Holy Spirit employed men as *instruments* to write" (*Enchiridion Biblicum* 25 [110], italics added). He explained this action of the divine author on the instrumental (human) authors as follows: the Holy Spirit "by a supernatural force so aroused and moved them to write and so assisted them as they wrote that they correctly conceived with the mind, faithfully willed to write down, and with infallible truth gave suitable expression to all that He commanded and only that" (*ibid.*).

The precise nature of this collaboration of divine and human authors has been the object of detailed theological speculation, particularly during the last century. The spur to such speculation came from the development of the experimental sciences and the archeologists' rediscovery of the ancient Near East. Until the last century practically no ancient Near Eastern literature was available with which to compare the Bible. Until the development of modern science, the pre-scientific conceptions of the ancient world (for example, of an earth-centered universe with a solid-dome sky) shared by the biblical authors with their contemporaries was still generally accepted. In its splendid isolation, and because it expressed the faith accepted throughout the Christian world, the Bible stood out as a unique book. It was God's book, containing His truth and, of course, no admixture of error. But all this has changed. The biblical writings are so strikingly like the rest of rediscovered ancient Oriental literature that many moderns refuse to recognize any difference whatever in them. And, of course, modern science has shown the untenability of many of the pre-scientific notions of the ancient world found in the Bible. Theologians have tried to reconcile the new findings with the Church's conception of the Bible as a unique book. Especially they have tried to reconcile the presence of incorrect views (like ancient ideas of the organization of the universe)

with the Church's teaching on the Bible's freedom
from error.

Several attempts made in the last century proved
false or inadequate. For example, it was suggested
that the biblical writings had God as author in the
sense that they contained revelations made by Him;
and the prerogative of inerrancy was limited to
these, other affirmations of the biblical authors being subject to error. In other words, God was author of only part of the Bible, and that part alone
was altogether free of error. This suggestion, of
course, was rejected.

From the discussion that began with this proposal a capital distinction gradually became clear:
the difference between inspiration and revelation.
Revelation means (God's) giving (or infusing) new
ideas or thoughts. Inspiration means (God's) mov-
ing a man to write a book. There seems to be no
reason why God cannot move a man to write a
book which does not contain any new revelations —
for example a book urging men to live up to an already known (religious) ideal.

Another outcome of the discussion over biblical
inerrancy seemed to be the conclusion that everything in the Bible comes entirely from God as it also
comes entirely from the human authors. This raised
the question: if everything comes from God, then
how can the human author be anything more than
a secretary? Late in the last century Cardinal J. B.
Franzelin, S.J., attempted to solve this problem by

ascribing the thoughts in the biblical writings to God (given by Him to the human authors) and leaving the choice of words to express these thoughts to the initiative of the human writers. But since this seems really to make God author of only part of the Bible and the human writers authors of another part, the proposal has been generally abandoned.

In an attempt to find a satisfactory solution to the problem of the co-operation of the divine and human authors, M. J. Lagrange, O.P., suggested the development of certain ideas St. Thomas Aquinas had presented in his study of prophecy. Pierre Benoit, O.P., has exploited those ideas. He recalls Aquinas' distinction between the *ideas* in any given judgment and the *light* by which the connection (or lack of connection) between the ideas is perceived. For example, in the judgment, "The sun is shining," "the sun" and "shining" are the two ideas involved, and the connection between the two is affirmed on the basis of the speaker's experience (looking out of the window) or the witness of another (if the speaker is blind, for example) or some other evidence. If God infuses (gives supernaturally) new ideas and the light to judge their connection (for example, "Father, Son, and Holy Spirit are one God"), we have revelation — the kind of revelation a prophet receives. If God infuses simply the light to perceive the connection between ideas already had elsewhere (for example, from experience), then

we have a supernatural judgment which may be
called "inspired" (produced in a unique way by
God and, therefore, divinely certain and correct),
though not "revealed." Biblical inspiration consists
in God's supernaturally producing not only such
judgments but also the determination to set them
down in writing, the choice of words, and all else
that goes into authoring a book. But it consists in
God's doing this in such way as not to deprive the
human author of complete freedom and full re-
sponsibility for this work. This makes both God
and the human author responsible for the entire
writing, and yet each in a different way. How God
can so determine the human author, however, and
still leave him free remains unanswered. The answer to this question will be given according to the
theologian's opinion on the broader problem of the
reconciliation of divine causality and all human
freedom.[17]

Karl Rahner, S.J., has noted that this and similar
theological explanations of inspiration leave many
questions about the Bible unanswered, though they
are intimately bound up with the inspired character of the book. For example, there is the problem
of the relationship between an inspired and therefore inerrant Bible and an infallible ecclesiastical

17 This is, of course, an extreme simplification of Benoit's position. For a full treatment see P. Synave and P. Benoit, *Prophecy
and Inspiration* (New York: Desclée, 1961), or A. Robert and A.
Tricot, *Guide to the Bible* (New York: Desclée, 1960), chapter I,
"Inspiration" by P. Benoit.

teaching authority, or between Scripture and tradition: does not one make the other unnecessary?
Or again there is the problem of the possibility of
inspired writings (Apostolic letters, for example)
that have been lost, the problem of how the Church
decided which books were inspired and which were
not, the problem of whether God could make new
revelations and inspire further books. Answers, of
course, have been offered for these questions by
theologians, but the answers do not flow from the
nature of the biblical writings *as inspired*. Hence,
Rahner has proposed a new approach.[18]

God's relation to the Church of the first Christian
generation is unique, since during that generation
the Church was still coming to be (just as a mother's
relationship to her child during pregnancy and child-
birth is different from what it is in the time that
follows).[19] He wills this first Christian generation
and what comes into existence during its time as
constitutive of the Church. Christians of later generations will be the Church insofar as they conform
to and continue the constitutive elements that came
into existence during the first — for example, insofar as they conserve diaconate and priesthood, insti-

[18] The following is an extreme simplification of Rahner's position. For a full presentation see K. Rahner, *Inspiration in the Bible*
(Freiburg: Herder, and Edinburgh-London: Nelson, 1961).

[19] The Church was not completely formed at the descent of the
Holy Spirit on Pentecost. To cite but one instance of additional,
post-Pentecostal development: the deposit of Revelation was not
complete until the end of the Apostolic generation — new public
revelations were possible until then.

tuted during those early years, or insofar as they conserve faith in the entire first-generation deposit of revelation. The New Testament writings form part of these elements constitutive of the Church. They are willed by God as the primitive Church's written expression of her Apostolic faith (to which, of course, future generations must conform). This unique act of God's willing the first-generation Church, *insofar as it regards the production of New Testament writings,* is inspiration. The inspired books are clearly authored by men and yet are also in an altogether unique sense God's. Rahner extends his thinking to the Old Testament writings by pointing out that they were willed by God to prepare for the Church and to retain validity for the Church and, therefore, are also in a sense a formative element of the Church (though antedating the first Christian generation). This theological explanation offers answers to the problems mentioned above based on the very nature of inspiration. Tradition and the teaching authority of the Church are neither limited to merely repeating the Bible nor simply independent of it, but must repeatedly refer to it (in particular to the New Testament) as the Apostolic generation's normative self-expression of the Church's faith. The Church decided which writings were inspired by deciding whether or not particular writings were really (the Apostolic generation's) expression of her faith. There can be no further public revelation or inspiration after the first

Christian generation since the constitution of the Church — the eschatological event — was completed then.

It is clear that these last two theological positions on inspiration are concerned with explaining how both God and the human composers can be authors of the same book, and not particularly with explaining the Bible's inerrancy. The reason is that the latter doctrine hardly poses any problem today. It is now universally recognized that the correctness or error of a statement does not depend on the face value of the words used. A metaphor (for example, Jesus' words to the Apostles in Jn. 15:5: "I am the vine, you the branches") or a hyperbole (for example, His words on the destruction of Jerusalem in Matt. 24:21: "There will then be such great tribulation as has never occurred since the world's beginning . . . and as will never occur again") must not be understood as bald observations of fact. Taken in that way, they are false: He is not a vine, and there have been sieges worse than that of Jerusalem. But taken as metaphor or hyperbole, they are true. In short, just as the difference between revelation and inspiration became clear in the last century, so the difference between making an affirmation and the way in which it is made — its literary form — became clear. An affirmation can be correctly described as true or false only if it is evaluated *in the sense in which it is made*. Biblical authors could well employ, for example, false pre-scientific ideas and even think them true without *affirming* them as factual but simply *using* them to give religious teaching — which, of course, it is the principal purpose of all the biblical writings to convey. Thus, for example, the author of Genesis 1 describes the creation of the universe in the way he conceived of it (solid-dome sky, etc.). However, he was interested in affirming not the construction of the universe but the (religious) fact that God created it. Or again, biblical writers could recount traditional stories that were inaccurate in many details without being guilty of affirming errors, because they (like other ancient Near Eastern historians) were not concerned with and had no intention of affirming factually accurate details but wanted to affirm through traditional accounts the meaning of some important event or occurrence.

Thus theological discussion of the Church's traditional (and defined) view of the Scriptures has been carried on against the background of the development of modern science and the rediscovery of the ancient Near East. It has gradually brought to light distinctions of great importance for a proper appreciation of the biblical writings. It presses on to a fuller understanding of their unique nature in order to come to a clearer appreciation of their unique message or content: the story of the divine self-revelation to men.